Death Knock: The Cosmic Tear

Book Introduction:

In the heart of the sprawling metropolis, where shadows whispered secrets and evil deeds thrived, emerged Death Knock. A figure wrapped in mystery, her ebony hair flowing like a river of darkness, Death Knock was not just a hero; she was a legend. In a world teetering on the edge of chaos, she stood as a beacon of hope, her every step shrouded in enigma and grace.

The city knew her as Death Knock, a name whispered in fear and awe. But who was she really? From whence did she come? None could answer. Her past was veiled, lost in the labyrinth of time. Some speculated she was a cosmic being, sent to maintain the delicate balance between light and darkness. Others believed she was a mortal touched by a sinister force, granting her extraordinary powers. Regardless of her origins, her purpose was clear: to battle the malevolent forces that crept in the night and protect the innocent from their clutches.

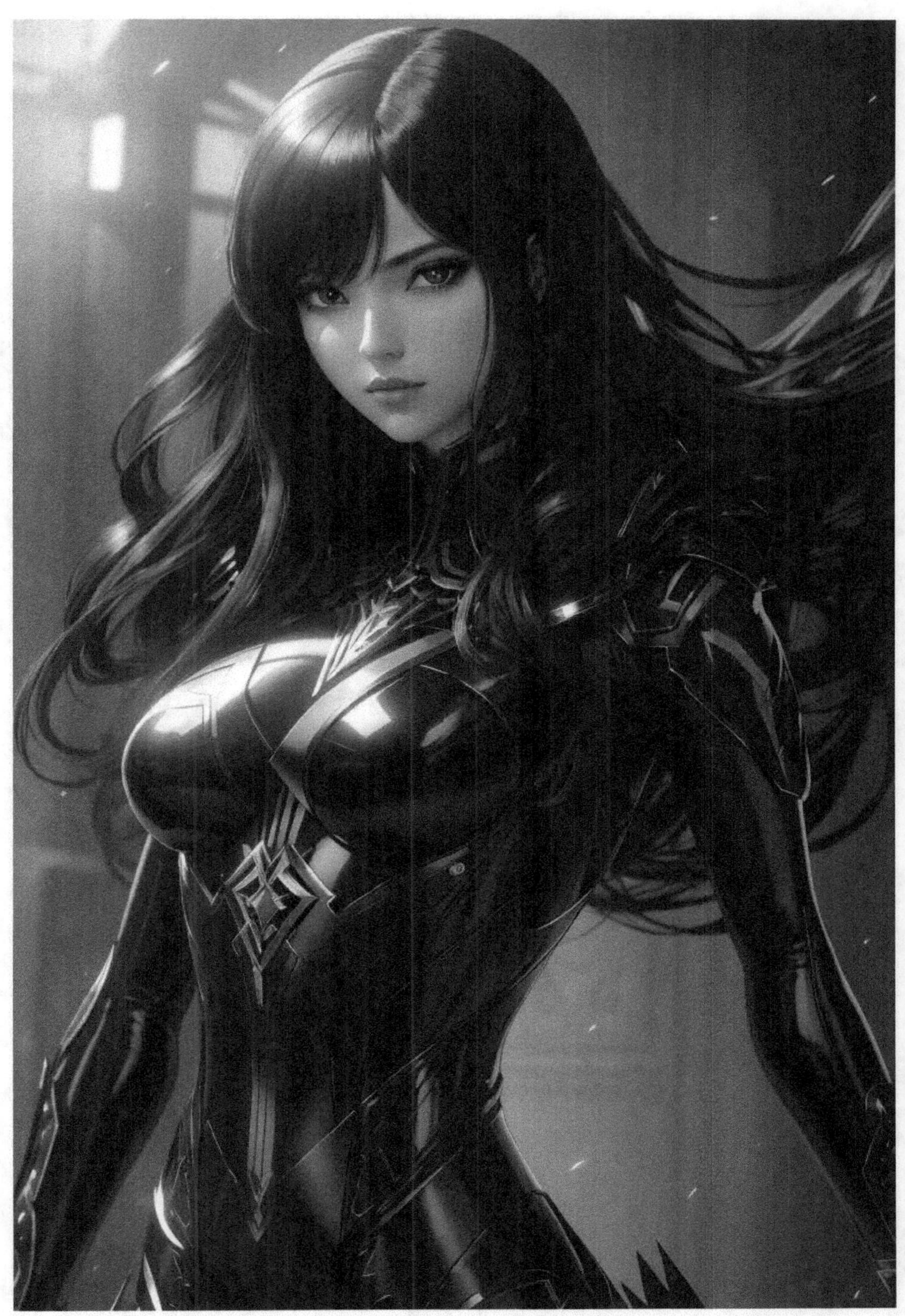

Chapter 1: The Awakening of Shadows

In the heart of the city, where neon lights painted the night in vivid hues and the pulse of life echoed through its streets, a darkness stirred. It was not an ordinary darkness but a sentient one, a shadow that slithered through the alleys and danced beneath the glow of the moon.

This shadow was not a mere absence of light; it was a presence, a malevolent force waiting for the right moment to reveal itself.

On this particular night, as the city slept beneath a blanket of stars, a cosmic phenomenon occurred. A meteor shower, a celestial ballet of stardust and fire, graced the sky. Unbeknownst to the city dwellers, this meteor shower carried with it an ancient force, a power as old as the universe itself. As the meteors streaked across the heavens, one of them veered off its destined path, guided by an unseen hand, and crashed into the heart of the city.

In the aftermath of the impact, a figure emerged from the cosmic dust, a silhouette wrapped in shadows and mystery. This figure, known as Death Knock, was no ordinary being. She was a convergence of cosmic energies and ancient prophecies, a guardian born from the collision of celestial forces. With each step, the ground seemed to tremble beneath her, and her eyes, the color of deep amethyst, gleamed with intelligence and purpose.

The city, unaware of the cosmic events unfolding in its midst, continued its slumber. But Death Knock knew. She sensed the impending threat, an ancient evil awakening from its eons-long slumber. With her supernatural senses, she followed the tendrils of darkness that snaked through the city, seeking the source of this malevolence.

In the depths of an abandoned cathedral, where shadows clung like cobwebs and silence reigned like a forgotten king, Death

Knock confronted the source of the disturbance. There, amidst ancient relics and faded frescoes, stood a sorcerer whose lust for power had driven him to dark depths. He had harnessed the fallen meteor's energy, believing it would grant him unparalleled power, unaware that he was merely a vessel for a force far beyond his understanding.

"You cannot comprehend the forces you've unleashed," Death Knock's voice echoed through the chamber, carrying the weight of cosmic inevitability. "The balance of this city, and perhaps the entire cosmos, is at stake."

The sorcerer, blinded by his ambition, scoffed at Death Knock's warning. With a wave of his hand, he unleashed a torrent of shadowy energy, thinking to overpower this enigmatic intruder. But Death Knock was no ordinary foe. With a flicker of her cloak, she melded into the darkness, becoming one with the shadows that surrounded her.

The sorcerer's attacks found no target as Death Knock emerged from the shadows, her presence now as ethereal as the night itself. With a touch, she marked the sorcerer, a cosmic sigil glowing ominously on his forehead. This mark rendered him vulnerable to her powers, a fact he realized too late.

In the ensuing battle, Death Knock displayed her mastery over shadows and celestial energies. Her movements were a dance of cosmic power, a ballet of light and darkness that left the sorcerer bewildered and defenseless. With a swift strike, she shattered his defenses, dispersing the stolen cosmic energies and banishing the ancient evil that had manipulated him.

As the sorcerer lay defeated, his eyes wide with terror and realization, Death Knock's eyes softened with empathy. "Your thirst for power led you astray," she said, her voice a melodic whisper. "Remember this moment, for it is a testament to the consequences of imbalance."

With those words, Death Knock vanished into the shadows, leaving the abandoned cathedral bathed in the soft glow of moonlight.

The city, still unaware of the cosmic battle fought in its midst, remained shrouded in silence.

But Death Knock's presence lingered, a subtle whisper in the night wind, a reminder that in the face of darkness, there would always be a guardian, a silent sentinel beneath the stars, ensuring that the cosmic balance endured.

And thus, the tale of Death Knock began, silent yet profound, in the boundless realms of the cosmos.

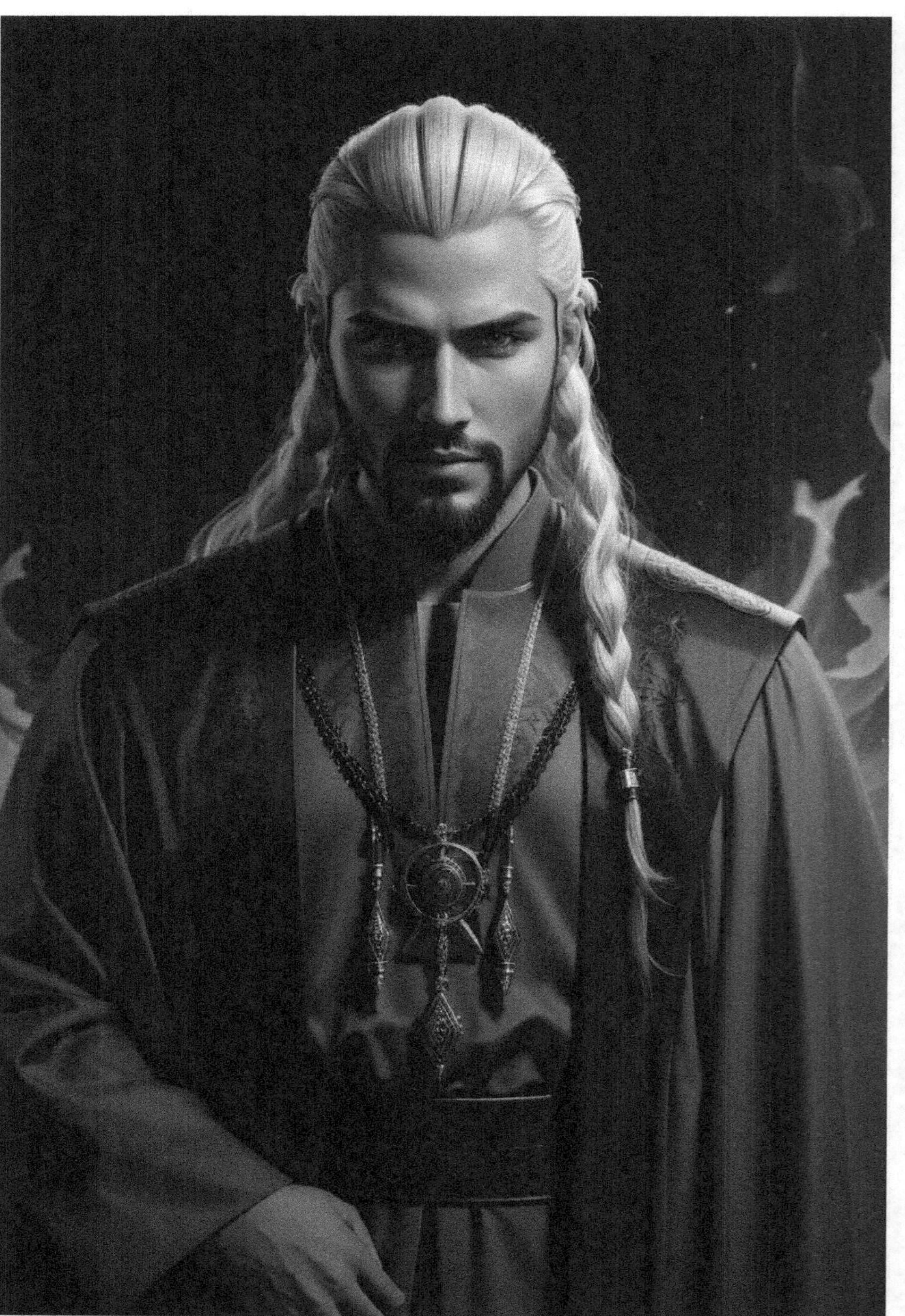

Chapter 2: Shadows of Deceit

In the wake of her initial confrontation, Death Knock's presence in the city became a whisper, a legend passed through hushed tones in the corners of dimly lit bars and among those who dared to venture into the realm of the supernatural. Unseen and enigmatic, she continued her silent vigil, ever watchful for the flicker of darkness that signaled an imbalance in the cosmic order.

One night, as the city's skyline glittered with the myriad lights of urban life, a series of mysterious disappearances sent ripples of fear through the community. People, young and old, began vanishing without a trace, leaving behind nothing but whispers of their existence. The police were baffled, unable to find any connections between the victims.

Death Knock, attuned to the cosmic energies, sensed a familiar malevolence at play. Her amethyst eyes narrowed with determination as she followed the tendrils of darkness that led her to an abandoned theater, its grandeur faded, but its aura still heavy with the weight of forgotten performances.

Inside the theater, Death Knock found herself in a realm of shadows. The air was thick with an unnatural darkness, and the walls seemed to pulse with an otherworldly heartbeat. There, she discovered a cult of shadow-worshipers, their eyes gleaming with fanaticism as they chanted ancient incantations.

Their leader, a charismatic yet twisted individual named Malachai, stood at the center of the congregation. He was harnessing the stolen life force of the missing people, intending to channel it into a dark ritual that would grant him unimaginable power. Unbeknownst to Malachai, his actions had drawn the attention of Death Knock, the silent guardian whose purpose was to protect the innocent from such malevolence.

"You tread a dangerous path, summoner of shadows," Death Knock's voice cut through the eerie silence of the theater, her cloak billowing like a cosmic tempest.

Malachai, believing himself invincible with the stolen life forces coursing through his veins, scoffed at her. "I am on the cusp of godhood! No one can stand in my way."

With a gesture, Malachai unleashed the stolen life forces, sending them hurtling towards Death Knock in a torrent of dark energy. But Death Knock was prepared. With a graceful movement, she summoned her mastery over shadows, melding into the darkness and allowing the energy to pass harmlessly through her.

Emerging from the shadows, Death Knock countered with a force of cosmic energy that engulfed Malachai. The stolen life forces recoiled, returning to their rightful owners with a gentle touch of Death Knock's hand, restoring the victims to consciousness.

Malachai, his power waning, tried to escape, but Death Knock was faster. With a swift movement, she incapacitated him, her touch sapping his strength until he fell to the ground, defeated and powerless.

"You sought power at the cost of others' lives," Death Knock's voice was stern, her gaze unwavering. "But true strength lies in protecting the vulnerable, not preying upon them."

With those words, Death Knock turned away, leaving the cultists in shock and Malachai in despair. The stolen life forces dissipated, returning the theater to its former state of eerie quiet.

The city, unaware of the cosmic battle fought within the abandoned theater, remained oblivious to the darkness that had momentarily threatened to consume it. Yet, somewhere in the depths of their subconscious, the people felt a subtle shift, a whisper of gratitude for the silent guardian who protected them from the shadows.

Chapter 3: The Shadows Resurge

In the depths of the city, where the echoes of forgotten alleys whispered ancient secrets, a sinister force stirred. It was a force reborn from the ashes of defeat, fueled by the remnants of Malachai's malevolent ambitions. The cultists, once scattered and defeated, had regrouped, their fanaticism burning brighter in the wake of their leader's downfall.

Malachai, his pride wounded and his thirst for power unquenched, delved deeper into forbidden knowledge.

He sought rituals and incantations that would grant him the strength to overcome Death Knock, the enigmatic guardian who had thwarted his previous attempt at godhood. His obsession with cosmic power bordered on madness, and the cultists, drawn to his charisma, followed him into the depths of the occult.

Their rituals grew darker, their incantations louder, and the shadows that danced around them became more than mere absence of light. Under Malachai's guidance, the cultists delved into the forbidden arts, tapping into forces that should have remained dormant. Unbeknownst to them, their actions sent ripples through the cosmic fabric, disturbing the delicate balance that Death Knock had sworn to protect.

Sensing the resurgence of dark energies, Death Knock emerged from the shadows once more, her eyes ablaze with determination. She followed the tendrils of malevolence to an abandoned mansion at the edge of the city, where the cultists had established their new sanctuary.

Inside the mansion, the air crackled with dark energy. The walls were adorned with esoteric symbols, and the cultists, their eyes feverish with zeal, chanted incantations that resonated with ancient cosmic forces. At the center of the ritual stood Malachai, his gaze defiant, his determination unyielding.

"You cannot escape the cosmic balance," Death Knock's voice echoed through the mansion, her presence a testament to the enduring power of the light.

Malachai sneered, his voice dripping with arrogance. "You think you can stop us? We have tapped into forces beyond your comprehension."

With a wave of his hand, Malachai unleashed the gathered energies, sending them hurtling toward Death Knock in a surge of darkness. But Death Knock was prepared. With a swift movement, she summoned her mastery over celestial energies, forming a barrier of light that deflected the dark onslaught.

The cultists, undeterred by their leader's failure, lunged at Death Knock, their eyes filled with fanatic fervor. But Death Knock was swift and agile, her movements a dance of cosmic grace. With each strike, she incapacitated a cultist, her touch sapping their strength until they fell, defeated and powerless.

Malachai, witnessing the defeat of his followers, unleashed his most potent incantation. Dark tendrils erupted from the ground, snaking toward Death Knock with the intention of ensnaring her. But Death Knock was not just a guardian; she was a master of shadows. With a flicker of her cloak, she melded into the darkness, becoming one with the very shadows that sought to bind her.

The cultists' cries of triumph turned into gasps of horror as Death Knock emerged from the shadows, her eyes ablaze with cosmic light. With a single touch, she marked Malachai, a cosmic sigil glowing ominously on his forehead. This mark rendered him vulnerable to her powers, a fact he realized too late.

In the final confrontation, Death Knock's mastery over light and shadows clashed with Malachai's dark sorcery. The mansion trembled with the cosmic forces at play, its very foundation threatened by the clash of opposing energies.

With a burst of celestial brilliance, Death Knock incapacitated Malachai, his dark powers proving no match for her cosmic mastery. The remaining cultists, their fanatic zeal shattered, fled in fear, leaving behind their fallen leader.

"You sought to upset the cosmic balance," Death Knock's voice was stern, her gaze unwavering. "But the harmony of the universe prevails over darkness."

With those words, Death Knock vanished into the shadows, leaving the abandoned mansion bathed in the soft glow of moonlight. The city, still unaware of the cosmic battle fought in its midst, remained shrouded in silence.

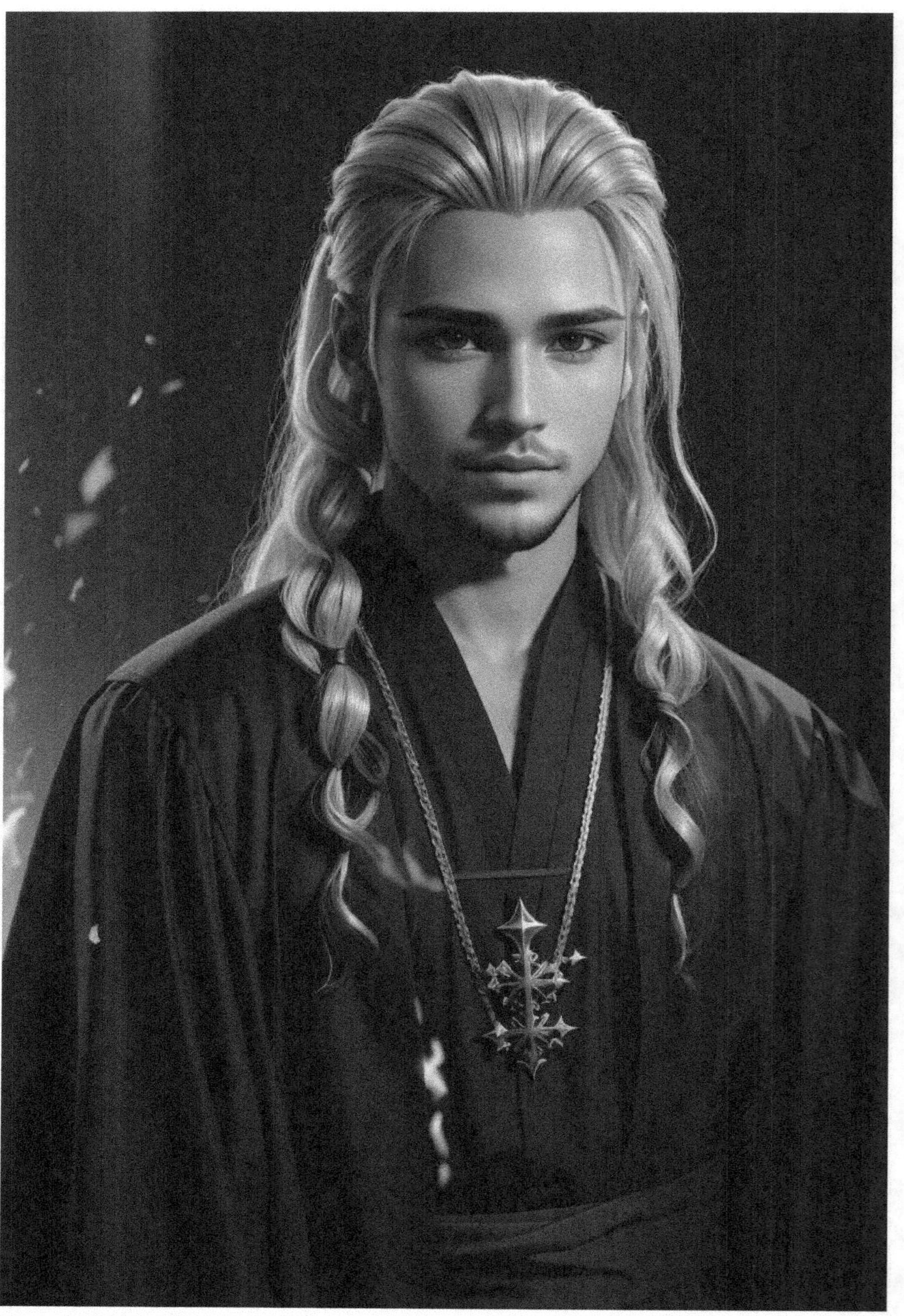

Chapter 4: The Shadows Conspire

In the aftermath of Malachai's defeat, a palpable tension hung in the air among his remaining followers. Fear and uncertainty gnawed at their hearts, but among them, a figure named Micah found resolve. Unlike his fellow cultists, Micah's mind was not clouded by blind fanaticism; he was a keen observer, one who had watched Death Knock's battles with Malachai with analytical eyes.

In the dim candlelit chambers of the cult's new sanctuary, Micah stepped forward, his voice carrying an air of conviction. "We have been blind to our leader's folly," he proclaimed, his words echoing in the hushed room. "But I have seen Death Knock's tactics, her strengths, and her vulnerabilities. I believe I have a plan that can defeat her."

His fellow cultists turned their eyes to Micah, their desperation mingled with newfound hope. Micah's plan was rooted in the knowledge he had gleaned from Death Knock's battles with Malachai, a strategic understanding that went beyond the blind aggression of his comrades.

The cultists gathered in secret, listening intently as Micah outlined his plan. His eyes glittered with a mix of fear and determination as he spoke, detailing Death Knock's reliance on shadows and celestial energies. He theorized that her powers were at their strongest in complete darkness, yet vulnerable when confronted with overwhelming light.

Under Micah's guidance, the cultists began to prepare. They crafted devices that emitted blinding light, designed to disorient Death Knock and strip away her advantage in the shadows. They studied ancient texts, seeking rituals that could counter her celestial energies. In their desperation, they even delved into forbidden arts, sacrificing their own humanity in the pursuit of power.

Meanwhile, Micah himself delved into the lore of ancient guardians and cosmic beings. He sought knowledge of Death Knock's origins, hoping to find a clue to exploit her weaknesses. His nights were spent poring over dusty tomes and deciphering cryptic scrolls, his mind consumed by a singular purpose.

One fateful night, as the moon hung low in the sky, Micah discovered a long-lost cosmic prophecy. It spoke of a guardian, Death Knock, whose powers were deeply intertwined with the cosmic balance. The prophecy hinted at a celestial artifact, the Cosmic Tear, said to be the source of Death Knock's powers. According to the prophecy, the artifact could be harnessed to weaken Death Knock's connection to the cosmic forces.

With newfound determination, Micah shared his discovery with the cultists. They embarked on a perilous journey to locate the Cosmic Tear, a quest that took them to the farthest reaches of the city and beyond. The artifact, hidden in a forgotten temple atop a mist-shrouded mountain, glowed with an otherworldly light as they found it.

Armed with the Cosmic Tear, the cultists returned to their sanctuary, their eyes filled with fervor. Micah, his hands trembling with anticipation, prepared the final ritual. The room pulsated with energy as the artifact resonated with Death Knock's distant presence.

The ritual began, the cultists chanting ancient incantations as Micah held the Cosmic Tear aloft. The room filled with blinding light, a stark contrast to the shadows that had once enveloped them.

Unseen forces surged through the air, echoing the cosmic dance of power.

In the midst of the ritual, Death Knock sensed the disturbance. Her eyes, like twin amethyst stars, widened with realization. She understood the danger posed by the cultists' plan, their desperate attempt to harness the powers of the Cosmic Tear against her.

With determination burning in her eyes, Death Knock emerged from the shadows, her cloak billowing like cosmic winds. She faced the cultists and their leader, Micah, her voice unwavering.

"You cannot control forces beyond your understanding," Death Knock's voice echoed with cosmic resonance. "The balance of the cosmos cannot be manipulated for your petty desires."

But Micah, his eyes ablaze with newfound confidence, pressed on. He chanted the final incantations, directing the power of the Cosmic Tear toward Death Knock. The room crackled with energy as blinding light engulfed her form.

For a moment, Death Knock seemed to waver, her silhouette flickering in the intense light. The cultists gasped in hope, their eyes wide with anticipation. But Death Knock's resolve was unyielding. With a surge of celestial power, she pushed back against the blinding light, her form glowing with an ethereal brilliance.

In a burst of cosmic energy, Death Knock shattered the cultists' ritual, dispersing the blinding light and rendering the Cosmic Tear inert. Micah fell to his knees, his confidence shattered, his hope eclipsed by despair.

"You underestimated the strength of the cosmic balance," Death Knock's voice was gentle, carrying a note of sadness. "It is a force

far beyond mortal comprehension, a tapestry woven with the threads of existence itself."

With those words, Death Knock vanished into the shadows, leaving the cultists in disarray. The room, once filled with blinding light, returned to its former dimness.

In the wake of their failure, the cultists were left to ponder the cosmic forces they had sought to manipulate. Micah, his eyes opened to the futility of their actions, vowed to atone for his mistakes. He disbanded the cult, guiding his fellow followers away from the dark path they had treaded.

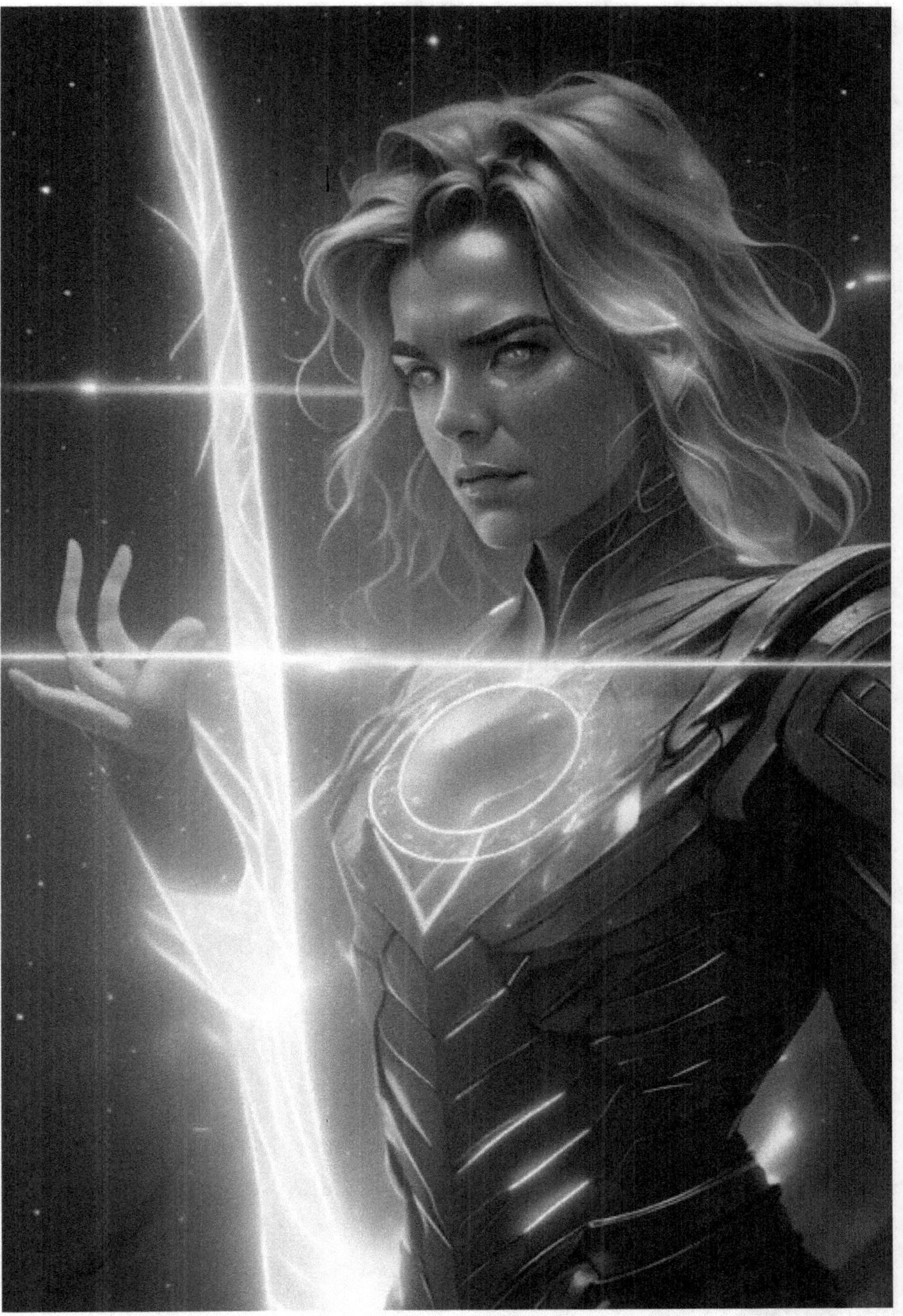

Chapter 5: The Cosmic Tear

In the aftermath of the battle with Micah and the cultists, Death Knock found herself changed. The remnants of the ritual, even though incomplete, had left a mark on her, a lingering weakness that seeped into her very essence. The Cosmic Tear, even in its inert state, had drained her of cosmic energy, leaving her feeling vulnerable and mortal.

The once effortless control over shadows felt strained, and the celestial power that once surged within her veins now flickered like a dying star. Death Knock, the silent guardian of the cosmic balance, had become mortal, her powers diminished to a mere echo of their former glory.

With determination burning in her eyes, Death Knock embarked on a quest to regain her strength. She ventured into the heart of the cosmos, seeking the wisdom of ancient cosmic beings and celestial sages. Through their guidance, she learned of a cosmic nexus, a convergence of energies that could restore her powers.

Her journey took her to the farthest reaches of the universe, where stars danced in cosmic harmony and nebulae glowed with ethereal light. There, amidst the interstellar tapestry, Death Knock discovered the Celestial Nexus, a radiant realm where the cosmic energies of creation and destruction intertwined.

As she entered the Nexus, she felt its energies embracing her, caressing her very soul. The cosmic beings within welcomed her, recognizing her as the guardian who had long preserved the balance of the cosmos. They bestowed upon her ancient knowledge, teaching her the secrets of the universe and the ways to harness the raw power of creation.

In the Nexus, Death Knock underwent a profound transformation. The cosmic energies flowed through her, knitting the fabric of her existence with threads of celestial light. She learned to channel the energy of stars, to command the forces of black holes, and to commune with cosmic entities whose names were whispered in the winds of distant galaxies.

With newfound wisdom and cosmic prowess, Death Knock returned to the mortal realm. Her eyes, once dimmed by weakness, now gleamed with the brilliance of a thousand stars. The shadows that clung to her form danced with renewed vitality, and the celestial energy within her pulsed with cosmic strength.

But the journey had come at a cost. The memory of her vulnerability haunted her, a reminder of the fleeting nature of her powers.

The Cosmic Tear, though inert, remained a threat. Its mere presence in the mortal realm was a disturbance in the cosmic balance, a blemish on the tapestry of existence.

Determined to rid the universe of this threat, Death Knock ventured back to the realm of mortals. She sought the guidance of ancient seers and cosmic scholars, hoping to find a way to cleanse the world of the Tear's influence. Her quest led her to forgotten temples and hidden libraries, where she delved into the lore of creation and destruction, seeking a solution to her predicament.

In her travels, Death Knock encountered allies and adversaries alike. Cosmic beings, aware of her mission, offered their aid, while dark entities, drawn to the Tear's power, sought to obstruct her path. Each encounter tested her newfound strength and resolve, pushing her to the limits of her cosmic abilities.

With unwavering determination, Death Knock confronted the remnants of the cult that had once sought to exploit the Tear's power. Their leaders, remnants of Micah's followers, had become corrupted by the Tear's influence, their minds twisted by its dark energies. Death Knock, now restored to her full cosmic might, battled them with a ferocity born of desperation.

In the midst of the battle, Death Knock's mastery over the cosmic forces shone brightly. She summoned celestial firestorms that consumed her enemies, and her shadows danced with the grace of supernovae, swallowing the corrupted cultists whole. With each defeated foe, she felt a fraction of her strength returning, a glimmer of hope in the face of darkness.

The final confrontation took place in the heart of an ancient temple, where the Tear's presence was strongest.

Death Knock faced the cult's corrupted leaders, their eyes glowing with malevolent power. The battle that ensued was a cosmic spectacle, a clash of titanic forces that shook the very foundations of the temple.

In a burst of celestial brilliance, Death Knock shattered the Tear's influence, banishing its dark energies from the mortal realm. The temple trembled, its ancient stones echoing the cosmic battle that had taken place within its walls. The cultists, freed from the Tear's corruption, fell to their knees in awe and gratitude.

With the Tear's influence eradicated, Death Knock felt a surge of cosmic energy coursing through her veins. Her powers, once diminished, now blazed with newfound intensity. The weakness that had plagued her was gone, replaced by a profound sense of purpose and strength.

But the experience had left its mark. Death Knock, the silent guardian of the cosmic balance, had faced her own mortality and emerged stronger. The memory of her vulnerability served as a reminder of the delicate balance that existed in the universe, a balance she vowed to protect with renewed vigor.

As she vanished into the cosmic winds, Death Knock knew that her journey was far from over. The universe was vast and ever-changing, filled with challenges and cosmic threats that tested the very fabric of existence. But she was ready. With her restored powers and unwavering determination, she would continue her silent vigil, ensuring that the cosmic balance endured for eternity.

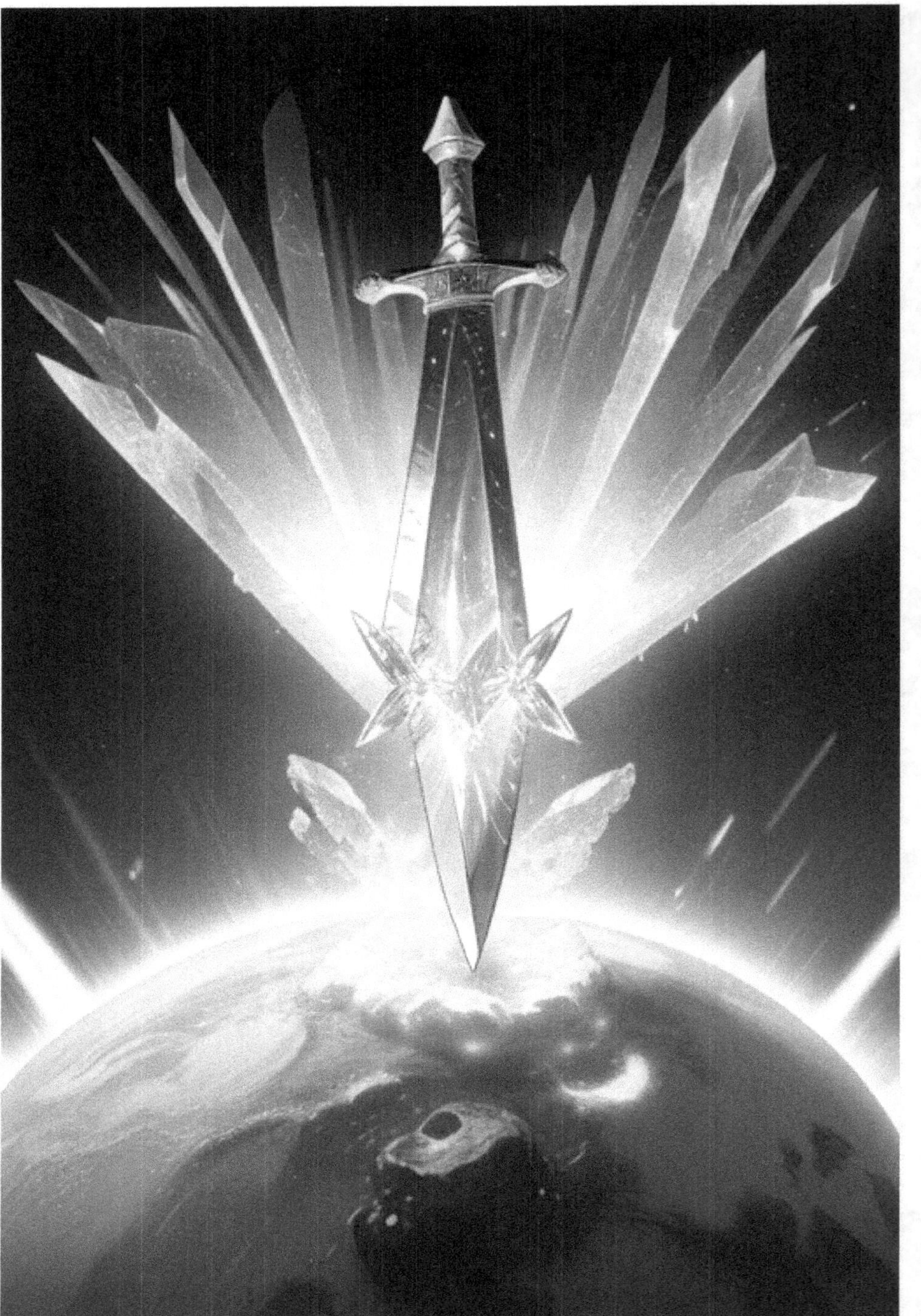

Chapter 6: Whispers of the Cosmic Tear

In the quiet aftermath of her victory over the cultists, Death Knock felt a peculiar unease settle within her cosmic core.

The eradication of the Cosmic Tear's influence had granted her renewed strength, but a nagging suspicion lingered in the depths of her consciousness. Unbeknownst to her, the Tear, though seemingly defeated, had found a way to restore itself, its essence shifting and evolving in the face of adversity.

The Tear's dark energies, once banished, had become subtle whispers in the cosmic winds. It learned from its previous failures, weaving a cloak of invisibility around itself, rendering it undetectable even to Death Knock's keen senses. In the silent corners of the universe, it plotted its return, biding its time until the moment was ripe to strike again.

With a newfound cunning, the Tear devised a way to call upon Death Knock's enemies, whispering promises of power and cosmic mastery to those attuned to its dark frequencies. Its tendrils of influence reached out across the stars, seeking out beings whose desires matched its own, drawing them into its malevolent embrace.

Unaware of the Tear's resurgence, Death Knock continued her vigil, patrolling the cosmic realms with unwavering determination. Yet, as she moved through the vastness of space, a sense of foreboding settled upon her. The shadows seemed to stretch a little longer, and the stars whispered secrets that eluded her understanding.

One fateful night, as she navigated the cosmic tapestry, Death Knock encountered a being unlike any she had faced before. Zephyr, a cosmic sorcerer, had fallen under the Tear's influence.

His once-benevolent heart was now corrupted by the promise of unlimited power, and he wielded dark energies with a mastery that sent shivers through the universe.

Their battle was fierce, a clash of celestial forces that illuminated the heavens with cosmic fireworks. Zephyr, empowered by the Tear's whispers, fought with a ferocity that took Death Knock by surprise. Shadows danced at his command, and bolts of dark energy lashed out like cosmic lightning.

Despite her newfound strength, Death Knock found herself hard-pressed to counter Zephyr's onslaught. The Tear's influence had granted him an advantage, a dark cunning that matched her own. With each strike, he weakened her resolve, testing the limits of her cosmic abilities.

In the midst of their battle, Death Knock realized the truth. The Tear had returned, its presence hidden from her senses, its whispers guiding her enemies. Determination blazed in her amethyst eyes as she faced Zephyr, her voice carrying the weight of cosmic inevitability.

"You are a pawn in a cosmic game," she said, her words echoing through the void. "The Tear's influence blinds you to the true balance of the universe. But I will show you the light that exists even in the darkest corners of existence."

With a surge of celestial energy, Death Knock unleashed her most potent abilities. Stars erupted from her fingertips, illuminating the cosmic battlefield with their brilliance. Shadows twisted and coiled around her, responding to her command with unwavering loyalty.

In the face of Death Knock's cosmic onslaught, Zephyr faltered. The Tear's influence wavered, its grip on his mind weakening under the onslaught of her power. With a final burst of cosmic energy, Death Knock incapacitated him, dispelling the dark energies that had clouded his judgment.

As Zephyr fell, his eyes cleared, and he looked up at Death Knock with a mixture of gratitude and regret. "I was blind to the truth," he whispered, his voice filled with remorse. "Thank you for showing me the way."

Death Knock's eyes softened with empathy. "The darkness can cloud even the brightest hearts," she said, her voice gentle like the cosmic winds. "But as long as there is light, there is hope. Remember that."

With those words, Death Knock vanished into the cosmic winds, her presence a reminder that even in the face of the Tear's cunning, there would always be a guardian, a silent sentinel beneath the stars, ensuring that the cosmic balance endured.

"In the vastness of the cosmos, balance is not a choice but a necessity," Death Knock's voice echoed through the universe. "I am the guardian of that balance, and I will not falter."

To Be Continued in Volume 2.........................